four

fourth child

poems by Megan Hall

ISBN: 978-0-9802729-0-1
© Megan Hall 2007

2nd impression 2008

First published in 2007 by Modjaji Books
P O Box 385, Athlone, 7760
modjaji.books@gmail.com

Edited by Robert Berold
Printed and bound in South Africa by Creda Communications (Pty) Ltd
Cover artwork: Hannah Morris
Book design by: Stuart-Clark & Associates cc

Acknowledgements

Other versions of some of these poems were published as follows: 'Darning' (*Imago, New Contrast*); 'Gunshot' (*New Coin*); 'Suicide notes' (*New Coin*); 'Real' (*Fidelities*); 'What love is' (*New Coin*, Litnet); 'Meeting at night' (*Imago*, Litnet); 'Anniversary' (*New Contrast*); 'To a friend, on getting older' (*Imago, Carapace*); '14' (*Carapace*); 'Face' (*New Contrast*); 'Dance hall' (*Carapace*).

Thank you from the author

To Colleen Higgs for her decision to publish this book, Robert Berold and Hugh Hodge for hearing some of these poems read for the first time, and Robert again for his editorial skill.

Also to certain people for their forbearance in being written about, directly or indirectly, which most writers probably cannot do without.

Contents

Darning

Not surreptitiously,
but so as to make the darns and patches
themselves the focus of light.

I hope to do this
over the hole in my soul
you made.

Gunshot

There seem to be so many movies, now,
where people get shot in the head.
The camera treats them all slightly differently.
Tarantino splattered the brains and bits of skull

over the interior of a car. The anti-heroes
are giving a lift to an innocent boy, someone they've just saved,
in fact, from another bunch of thugs.
Then one of them shoots him by mistake.

The humour seems to lie in the cleanup operation,
in their chagrin at the mess, and in the nuisance
of having bits of identifiable bone
sprayed around their car. Perhaps it had just been cleaned.

Sam Mendes, on the other hand, simply
shows us the gun in position at the back of the head –
nothing accidental about it – then pans slowly
over the breakfast table. The motif

of the red roses makes an appearance,
and then the camera focuses
on the white mortuary-like tiles on the wall,
which will shortly be splattered with blood,

and one smallish chunk of gore,
but no bone or bits of skull this time. Later,
the home movie fundi, a beautiful boy with thick eyebrows,
leans over the body and the breakfast table

covered in a thick layer of enviscousing blood
(skinning over just like custard
or hot milk), and proclaims it beautiful.
It is beautiful: the camera is at table-height

and I almost expect to see the blood meniscus
as it laps thickly at the table edge, before dripping to the floor.
The father's head lies on its side, eyes open,
no wound showing, looking peaceful.

Through all this, I think of my father:
how he sees these movies, what they say to him,
what they remind him of. I could ask him,
make him re-live those moments:

finding his wife in the passage of their house
with two gunshot wounds to her head,
one voluntary, the other 'a simple reflex movement
of the hand', according to the medical report,

and afterwards being able to see, and being able to hear,
and not being able to forget, just how the blood ran,
                                        the bits of bone fell.

Suicide notes

'It may be simply that those who write them
care more about being remembered.'
I know I didn't say much, but I'm in a hurry.

1

There are only 5 kinds of suicide note, the experts say.
In the first kind, the writer blames someone
for reaching this point. *If you hadn't let me down,*
I wouldn't be feeling so bad.

In the second kind, the writer denies that the obvious reason
is the cause. *Just because my wife left me doesn't mean this*
has anything to do with her.

Then the third kind, where the writer both blames someone
and denies that this is the case. *What you did hurt me, but that isn't*
why. I just don't have a reason to stay.

The fourth kind mentions an insight suddenly received.
Last night I realised all my chances had slipped away,
would never come again. There seemed no point. I want to die.

The fifth kind contains no explanation at all, only instructions
for the dispersal of property. *My rings must go to Susan, but the*
                                                        large tablecloth
I want Mrs Next Door to have.

2

I wonder how the expert would classify your note, and why.
The expert doesn't say much about why, or what people who read
these notes
feel when they get them. I suppose it's implied.

I can't say I know; I'm only a second-hand reader, too many years
too late. I couldn't help the expert with his investigations
and I'm not going to give him your note for his collection.

Still, reading the photocopy the police let us have
sprouts tears in me; pity and fear blended together.
(Maybe a dusty police file holds the original still?)

I am the property to be disposed of in your note;
it may have been the first time you owned me in this way,
then immediately bequeathed, handed me over,

intact, to the next generation.

Real

I make myself real by sneezing.
I dream of the myth of handkerchiefs, blue and green,
embroidered flowers in the corners. *Did they bleed?* I ask.
Did they gasp? White emanations from the heart.

I swing these butterflies of dry sleep around me like swords.
They keep away the looks that want to peel me
like a willow wand and shoot me far. *Keep them away*, I say,
I'm not for you to split and shred.

I hold my shell, a coracle on the beach. Outside
I'm brown and dry. Maybe no one will want me.

Between my ears: cups and saucers, outer space,
a blackness where stars have never shone.

Between my legs: old words come out at night,
take shape, cast shadows.

What love is

heat
bleeding gums
hot pink and bright red together

*

orange geraniums
the oven element glowing
the long scar under your wrist

Meeting at night

The room smells of catpiss, jonquils and narcissus,
an edge of smoke and sweat.

You are still inside me, our lips touching but not kissing,
your head on my shoulder.

How many more times are we going to do this? We get older,
stained with the meetings and leavings of other bodies.

Tomorrow or next year, I will leave, you will leave –
we'll write letters across this country, and others,

letters that don't mention our infidelities with each other:
on paper we are faithful, if not celibate.

Anniversary

It burst into the wall above our bed –
a rocket, a bullet, a streak of light.
The wall shook and crumbled, falling away.
The roof took off in fright,
flapping wings of mouldy red tiles.

In the middle of the city, our bed:
dogs barking, drunks stumbling home.

This is where the last two years have brought us:
back to a city street

and you,
trying not to hold my hand.

To a friend, on getting older

Beloved, unlike me, you're getting older.
As the sun draws wrinkles with a steel-nibbed pen
and catches the backs of your ears,
and the women with which you enliven your nights,
and afternoons, are younger and younger,
and you older and hairier,
I hope you grow to be a really mean motherfucker,
and travel far, but stay close, and regret me always.

14

I've felt the secret only this body can bring:
the swelling, the uncertainty, the hot nights,
lover curled round me like an arc, a parabola,
the sun setting slowly on an autumn day.

I've seen the pictures on the screen,
rolled the knowledge over like a pebble on my tongue,
trying to find purchase, trying to find
an entry, some rough space.

The egg refuses to be known, whole and perfect to itself.
Mine popped from its seedpod, travelled down the combed womb,
met a thousand travellers. In an instant,
as the tingling sparks still ran through me
and the pearls of sweat globed on your nose and forehead:
$x + (x \text{ } or \text{ } y)$.

Wolwekloof

Lizard tongue, you are still in my dreams.
I remember   the hot fingers of amphetamine,
and your grey reptilian tongue;

                        being discovered on the hillside,
dress so rumpled, it looked like
the creases had been ironed in.

The dead man and his lover

1
His lover's eyes are violet-ringed. Giggling and swaying,
she leaves the church in her thin grey vest and black jeans.
My long black skirt and white silk blouse make me cringe:
dressed like a mourner for someone who didn't know my name.

A little chanting; some words in Greek; the priest reappears
from behind the golden screen. The coffin's open
but I don't go up, to ask for blessings or to give them,
don't look. I am afraid of the dead man.

Instead, I watch his parents in their grief, wonder if they think
that we're to blame, if they even know we're here.
Though their dark eyes see the church, see the standing people
                                                in the pews,
the cold body's what they take in, what they try to understand.

There's no family at the wake in Roseberry Road.
As I bum a cigarette, draw the smoke in deeply, someone
tells rude jokes about the dead. I watch the dead man's lover.
Screwing up her eyes against the smoke, she looks normal, smiles.

Still I don't know what to say to her; only know I should feel shocked.
Does she know he isn't coming back? –
Maybe none of us do. But later we go home and talk again
about the first one of us dead.

2

The lover speaks

Nico, Nico, what have you done to me?
The sky has gone inky black and you will never return.
You searched too long for the bursting stars,
illumination, the horizon's edge. Where is your body now?

The poppies the colour of walls and conchs
have wilted because of you, have wilted since Friday.
Last week I saw the tulips: their mouths were red,
their tongues were yellow, with the tip burnt black.

They spoke of agony to anyone who would listen.

Fourth child

1

To my grandmother
On the 49th day, God was kind, and made me your fourth child.

I don't believe in God, but I believed in you.
At 55, you took me in and made me
in the image of your other children,

as closely as you could.

2

April is the cruellest month. I should never call the day my mother
left 'kind'.

Only 49 days of motherhood, then she was gone.

The years go by, her image fades,
the colours leached, the edges frayed,
but the day remains, an anniversary kept

most years, but not commented on.
She took the words we needed with her.
Though I sift her ashes, I won't find them, know they're gone.

Seed

Deep within me is a seed.
You cannot reach it by probing.
One day perhaps, with the right feeding,
it will sink a root, burgeon a flower,
and its poisonous shadows will appear on my skin.

Who can be nearer in kin than a daughter
to a mother? Half the genes, the same sex,
a general expectation of looking alike.
But how far do I to want to push this, daughter of a suicide
who worked as a secretary and wanted to dance?

This seed's an inheritance I can't refuse,
a vine that could wrap itself around my life,
producing crazy flowers as it goes, just like the Bongleweed.
But mine's not the only one. Flowers from these seeds
bloom everywhere, sprout unexpectedly in strange places,

fruit themselves with shame and ruined weekends.
No, my seed's not alone; but too often we who remain
are left alone, hoping spring will not come.

Face

Of course it's vanity to choose to sit
right here by the square of silver-backed glass.
I cannot help looking, poring over
what I have grown up with, what has grown.

Hair is cut square and straight across my forehead,
close around the ears, shorn to the hairline
at the back. The same face looks out
of my pre-school photograph.

My eyes watch me as they never did then.
I cannot decide whether they or the rest of my face is mask.
Impassive, my mouth shows, then denies expression,
looks fuller on the left, sharper on the right. Perhaps it is.

Perhaps only the light, falling to cut my face
from hair to chin, falls unevenly. From here it looks
as if I'd have a profile – a lie. Nature stinted on my chin,
which falls a little too quickly to my neck.

A wavelet, soft and rolling, not a breaker. Still,
there's determination in the blankness of the eyes,
highset under a pair of forties eyebrows.
Two dark half-circles mimic the lines of hair,

but below my eyes. The nose is small, with little
elevation. Later, when I'm older, perhaps it will've grown,
become a Nose, dignified, aquiline. Or perhaps,
renegade, it will be one of the few that don't grow,

and all attempts at serenity at sixty will be flouted
by my nose, retroussé and freckled. You never know
which parts of you incline to treachery, which will raise
the flag of their own republic. These incipient frownlines

are even, true, but I have only one dimple
and the trench from nose to lip, though deep, is slanting.
The ears that held my glasses held them skew.
Now I wear lenses, the first additional pieces. They lie

like thin ice over a pond, giving a pool-like glitter
to the green-glass bits that are my vision. Sadly,
I look better blank than smiling. Humour holds
no symmetry or decorum, and these I need for order and
                                        patterning,

line by line, colour by colour, in the mirror.

Blame the ocean

Expanded from song lyrics by Stewart Bernard and Marjolaine Rouault

I've been washed up on your beach before
by waves that've kissed another thousand shores.
Then I got the message: you are self-contained.
If I'm here, blame the ocean, blame the waves.

CHORUS: Oh, I don't care what you do.
Just tonight I will have you,
pretend that you are mine.

I've been stranded at your door, alone;
again I'm waiting though your heart is stone.
You rose up from the waves just like a dream of mine.
If I'm here, blame the ocean, blame the waves.

CHORUS

BRIDGE: You're Scylla to my Charybdis, baby.
There's our love just sailing by.
Suck it down, or suck it dry.
This destruction gets us high.

We stare across the straits, the waters roar.
Think about feeling lonely just once more.
The lights go out, the rolling waves rush in.
If I'm here, blame the ocean, blame the waves.

CHORUS

I've been hungry for your kisses salty
and so sweet, but you were out of reach.
Now waves draw back, taking me with them to the deep.
If I'm here, blame the ocean, blame the waves.

CHORUS

Your smile that hooked right through me, to the quick,
how could I know it hid a thousand lies?
The birds have flown away; it's winter now and cruel.
If I'm here, blame the ocean, blame the waves.

CHORUS

How is it that I still want more of you,
when I know that pain is what you give
and give again, just like the endless waves on shore.
If I'm here, blame the ocean, blame the waves.

Leaving you

I thought I'd know if this was love
from the way it felt when we said goodbye
(as though I hadn't proved it to myself
with a hundred other goodbyes).

I thought I'd know if this was the final, the only love,
but I expect I'll only know this when it ends.

That morning in the sunlight, your leaving everywhere,
was temporally living and temporary despair.

You move fast

She's afraid to show her smile,
hides it and won't look up.

The smile is triumphant, pleased with itself,
it cannot believe its luck.

But luck's not allowed to happen to her:
she shouldn't be happy when he's sad.

He phones her to remind her of this,
to tell her how much he's hurt himself.

Of course, he doesn't put it quite like that.
He tells her   she's hurting him,

he can't believe, after everything,
she's hurting him this way.

She feels guilty. Even at 2 and 3 in the morning,
she doesn't put the phone down.

She wishes he could be happy too,
find someone new.

She doesn't tell him   his eyes were cold,
his words heavy as boots

pacing the room. She doesn't remind him
her skin split with tears.

Instead, she listens.
Admits, though she doesn't want to,

her new lover is there with her,
asleep in her bed.

'You move fast,' he says.
She doesn't contradict him.

The disappearance of the dead

For my mother: M H K
10.10.1940–16.4.1972

1
Where do they go, the dead?

The stories speak of triple-headed hell-hounds with open maws,
burning pyres, towers where the vultures come,
the sad wandering of ghosts in never-nether-worlds.

But you have seeped away into the world;
I cannot find you. Perhaps if I could look
with my father's eyes, I'd see you in the mirror.

Or if your mother hadn't thrown away
the reels that captured you, I could've seen you move.
But there's no chance of that, and anyway,

I want to see you for myself,
not through the filter of someone else.

2

All this suggests a presence you can't have.
For the cremated, the unspoken,
there's no grave to visit, no place to stand and think:

She's here below. Here people stood,
watched the coffin being lowered,
said prayers, threw in soil that landed with a rattle on the lid.

Comforted each other, went home for cake and tea,
then went on grieving: the first Christmas, the first birthday alone,
an empty place each evening, an empty chair.

Friends coming by, looking sorry, speaking her name,
offering to take the children for a night,
bring round a pot of stew –

But here I must break off.   There are no *children* in this case,
only me, and even in a fantasy, I can't picture the life that this implies:
dinner every evening, then TV; being looked after by my dad;

my mother's name spoken in the course of conversation
– with sadness, with regret – but spoken all the same.
This was your mother's favourite sauce; that kind of thing.

It couldn't happen.   The children of suicides don't get
this kind of solicitude. They get another kind: the kind
that watches over them with loving, tender, and careful, eyes,

just in case there's something to *inherit* after all.
No, better to say nothing, better to *keep it quiet.*
Encourage everyone to pretend that nothing's missing,

that there's nothing to miss, everything's all right.

3

What's the answer here? How can I bear a grudge against those
who gave me love, with a sense of taint, love
beyond themselves and their limitations?

4

To my mother, again
A suicide cannot be buried in a churchyard. So I think of you
lingering in the outer reaches, sacrament-less, far from grace,
like Tess's sad daughter, and her wooden cross.

Ground away into the soil, fragments and sensations
frittering away like dust on the wind,
slowly eaten by the moths of forgetting.

Yet you remain, while time holds,
                              mother.

Love is a habit

Love is a habit, like brushing your teeth or cleaning the bath.
And if love is a habit, is grieving one too? What shall I replace
the habit of loving and grieving you with?
                                        (A habit built up slow,
like the accretions on a pearl, grey and baroque and expensive;

or the gloss on a dining table, hours of elbow grease and polish;
or skin sloughing off imperceptibly, renewed from beneath;
or the silent unfurling of a baby, cell by cell.)
                                        (But
growth in the womb is by division, not addition; by one simple cell

splitting and replicating itself a million million times, till suddenly
                                        some know:
to shape a nose, and nose hairs, and a channel to the back of the mouth
that is slippery, and a tongue with nodules for tasting,
and teeth that are hard, but living.)
                        Love is a habit, and grieving one too.

But I want to hold on to the grieving as a way of holding on to you.
That first Sunday without you, the September sky was cold and empty,
despite the jasmine struggling to bloom.

I'd never lived a day without you in the world;
now the city for me was empty.
It hardly seemed possible.

Who gave us this gift?

1

Who gave us this gift, this most painful, unwanted gift
that still we must be thankful for – you and I?
Who gave us this death that took you away, so suddenly,
from me, and me from you?

Is it wrong to think of all the years of roast meat, crispy potatoes,
that had narrowed your arteries to winding lanes?
The extra baggage you carried doggedly for 60 years
– it got you in the end. You fell soft into the corridor.

Down on your knees so broad and beautiful when we played horsey
in the kitchen, you broke your fall a moment but could not stop.
The wrapping came off the gift; it was revealed.

When they had lifted you gently onto the bed,
covered you with your pink duvet,
I held your hand, taking from it unashamedly all I could:

the fingerprints rubbed smooth, knuckles just so,
skin yielding, soft and old and loose.
No other hand could do.

2

Clearly not your death, the gift you gave me was love; love
that made me know you knew I loved, and was loved by, you
– no need to wish I'd said it sooner, differently or more often.

That long slow path across the pass of death,
that Jimmy told me of so many years ago:
you won't be kept back from the crossing by my regrets:

we're clear. I loved you the best way I knew how
but not only now that you're not here.

Seams

For my grandmother

Her love is in the seams, the lengths of lace,
the afternoons spent being patient,
while I wasted another length of material,
attempting a pattern beyond my skill.

Her love is in the dresses I've outgrown but can't toss out,
each piece of each finished dress,
cut out on the floor as she bent over from the waist,
flat feet padding over fabric, rustling pattern paper.

In this demure dove-grey, made for my first job,
thin black ribbon at the collar, tied in a bow.

In the last dresses she made me, crepe-chiffon,
with full-circle sleeves and rolled necklines,
one a dusky faded pink, the other
autumn-yellow, falling leaves.

Star walk
Kirstenbosch Botanical Gardens

I choose a night walk, drag my dad along, my first birthday after
                                                                    her death.
We're the family we've got now, here in the south.

The stars beckon me, as we walk to where kind astronomers
have mounted their telescopes, prepared to share them even with us,
to whom the idea that *the sun is a star* seems strange and unnatural.

I lie on my back on the grass, and insects walk up the legs of my
                                                                    trousers
and bite me with small jaws. I am surprised they can open them
                                                                    wide enough.

After the scruffy anecdotes of the guide, star talk for real; real stars.
There are Canopus, and double Alpha Centauri like coupled
                                                        diamond shards.
I have never met these stars before, nor single Beta, red Sirius.

Small but clear, Saturn appears in my telescope's field,
a perfect luminous sticker for the ceiling.

Then the moon, with its scarred surface like an acned boy, but
                                                                    bright cream.
The stars and planets are bees in the night, each sun humming,
attracting and swarming, hot in the silent fields of sky.

Ticking

A house full of relics is what I'm living in,
heaped high to the ceiling, piled deep on the floor,
cutting out the light, blocking the door.

A house full of relics – bits of shell, stuffed heads,
tired old watches, too small clothes,
the smell of naphtha burning my nose.

But life's ticking stronger, the ticks resonate,
the rooms must be cleared, parcelled up, pulled into shape,
the relics pushed aside into corners, onto shelves:
so they can look on our lives but talk only to themselves.

Dancing on Robben Island
after a visit to KwaMashu Museum, Durban, March 2004

1

Govan Archibald Mvuyelwa Mbeki, born 1910,
of the Mfengu people, and the Zizi clan,
married Epainette Moerane.

Between 1933 and 1937, he read
penny Lenin texts bought at
The People Bookshop in Braamfontein.

He was 'a ballroom dancer of some repute'.
Together, 'they danced the quick step and the tango
at a club they started in Durban.

Later, alone in his prison cell
on Robben Island, he would rehearse those steps,
and imagine: Ma Mofokeng,

smiling in his arms.'

2

In her navy and black clothes,
Epainette feists through her glasses at the camera.
Her demeanour says, *No compromise.*
Says, *I am here in Idutywa to stay.*

No matter that her husband
(yes, they're still married),
the well-regarded Govan, has gone to Cape Town
to live a life of urban ease.

Her glance still says: *Here
there is something I can achieve.*

Cesaria live
27 March 2005

As she turns to the crowd, the hands clapping or waving,
the cameras and the lights,
her eyes say, *Maybe even this will pass, it's too late, so late.*
I will go back to singing in bars, barefoot,
the flare of fame will go.

Her eyes don't ask, *Why couldn't I have arrived here*
when I was young, and beautiful,
and could shimmy in a thin dress
and kick my heels?

They say, *My ancestors were slaves,*
stolen from this continent on whose southern tip I now stand.
Pain, pain is what I understand.

Her band throws in some jaunty numbers
(the violinist's cheerful, the backing singer too),
but the true melodies are those in minor keys.

Obrigada, she says, small and old under the lights.
A mañana.
Thank you. Until next time.

Dance hall

After a flying visit to New Zealand, July 2005

In the ephemera of a dance hall exhibition
at the National Library, Wellington
>   *dance cards filled in in spidery*
>   *copperplate,*
diaries of young girls trying not to be provincial, dresses and gloves
I'm unreasonably disappointed

at not finding evidence of my grandparents' dancing life.

Like Agnes and Don Manunui
>   *pictured left, in zooty two-button*
dinner jacket and belted white frock
they met at a dance somewhere near Napier.
Across the dance hall, she saw him laughing.

His teeth were white and even.
Her dress was home-made but backless and daring.
And they danced.
>   *Yes sir, that's my baby, no sir, don't mean maybe.*

Kiss

I bring all of myself to this kiss
  on the back of your neck
  as you work,
  where the hair feathers down onto your warm back,
  below the collar line.

the men I have said *no* to, and those I've said *yes* to,
  the long nights working, or dancing,
  the muddled, two-forward-one-back path
  to some sort of centre
  the best of myself I can offer, just under the skin

and you nod,
pursuing your own thoughts.

Your red and secret lips

Last night while you slept, or lay, pretending to sleep,
the light from the streetlamp fell on your bristly head,
shorn by a barber now far away, yet only yesterday.

In sleep, your eyebrows, prominent and emphatic,
are at rest. Below your nose, a small space
empty of moustache, then the delicate

and exceedingly beautiful
point of your upper lip,
almost rolled into a ball.

Lips that I've taken and tasted like sushi,
or a dead man's finger,
(jags of teeth, your demanding tongue);

lips that I've rolled between mine
like a stone rolled in water,
current flashing.

Wanting

Wanting's a powerful word.
I don't want to be left wanting,
want to be unafraid enough to want.

Wanting puts your heart out on a string,
trawling for the thing that's wanting you.
There's no hook, except maybe forever.

Wedding

1

We tell my dad, we're getting married.
It's a strange time, of emotion, and emotion denied.

How do we work it out, this strange new life?
Do what is right for us, find our own way
in the maze of expectations?

We find help from unexpected places.

2

No shade, not even a wisp,
but he raises her, my other parent, his dead wife.

In her empty wedding dress, green sash,
my mother makes her empty presence known,
living in our words, quietly.

For this I've waited all my life: those missing, those missed.

Notes to the poems

'Suicide notes' (pages 14–15): a piece published in the *New Yorker* suggested there were five types of suicide note; unfortunately, neither the issue number nor date is known.

'Dancing on Robben Island' (page 43–44): *Part 1:* The text in quotation marks is taken directly from the KwaMashu Museum display. No author is acknowledged there. *Part 2:* Epainette (1916–) and Govan Mbeki (1910–2001) were both stalwarts of the struggle. Their son, Thabo Mbeki, is the current president of South Africa.

'Your red and secret lips' (page 48): the title is borrowed from Patrick Cullinan's poem 'The bowl of tulips'.

Notes on the author

Megan Hall was born and grew up in Cape Town, and studied English and Latin at the University of Cape Town. Since 1995, she has worked in the publishing industry and is currently publisher for dictionaries and school literature in English at Oxford University Press Southern Africa.

Her poetry has appeared in various local journals since 1991, as well as the school anthology *Worldscapes*. A short story is forthcoming from Botsotso and an essay of hers was included in *Leaves to a Tree*, edited by Robin Malan. She has also edited poetry and fiction for *New Contrast*, and taken part in both *Young Voices* (the 2004 South African Online Writers' Conference hosted by Litnet) and the 2005 *Crossing Borders* programme, a British Council-sponsored writer's mentorship. She lives in Cape Town with her partner and a cat.